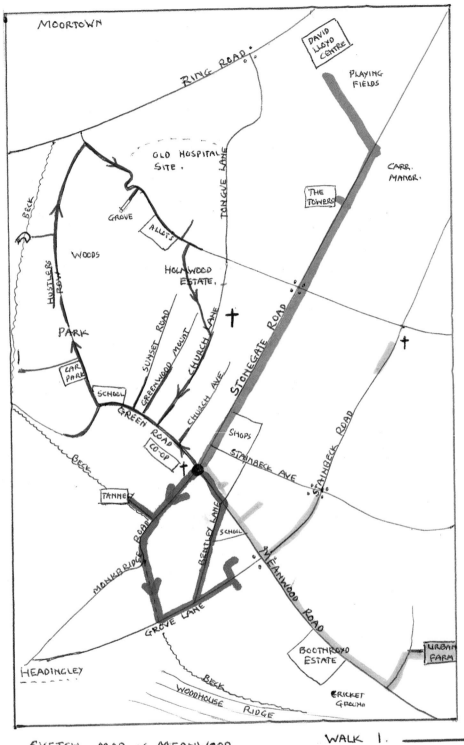

MOORTOWN

RING ROAD

DAVID LLOYD CENTRE

PLAYING FIELDS

CARR MANOR

OLD HOSPITAL SITE.

TONGUE LANE

THE TOWERS

BECK

GROVE

ALLOTS

WOODS

HOLMWOOD ESTATE.

HUSTLERS ROW

PARK

SUNSET ROAD

GREENWOOD MOUNT

CHURCH LANE

CHURCH AVE

STONEGATE ROAD

STAINBECK ROAD

CAR PARK

SCHOOL

GREEN ROAD

CO-OP

SHOPS

STAINBECK AVE

BECK

TANNERY

BENTLEY LANE

SCHOOL

MONKBRIDGE ROAD

MEANWOOD ROAD

GROVE LANE

BOOTHROYD ESTATE

URBAN FARM

HEADINGLEY

BECK

WOODHOUSE RIDGE

CRICKET GROUND

SKETCH MAP of MEANWOOD

SHOWING THE FOUR WALKS.

WALK 1.
WALK 2.
WALK 3.
WALK 4.

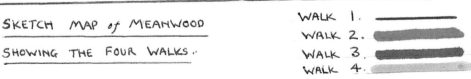

THE MEANWOOD VILLAGE ASSOCIATION PRESENTS

MEANWOOD
IN
PICTURES

Sunrise on 1st January 2000 from King Alfred's Castle.

VOLUME 3 — THE YEAR 2000

Compiled by
PETER BEWELL

Assisted by
ANNE BURGESS, BRYN EVANS and DOREEN WOOD

Published by
M.V.A.Publications

95, Green Road
Meanwood
Leeds LS6 4LE

First published 2007

ISBN 978 0 9547946 3 7

Printed and bound by
Smith Settle Printing and Bookbinding Ltd
Gateway Drive, Yeadon LS19 7XY

ACKNOWLEDGEMENTS

All the photographs in this book were taken by the following volunteer amateur photographers during the year 2000.

Peter Bewell
Paul Bound
Bryn Evans
Brian Glassby
Ian Jackson
John Whalley
Doreen Wood

The Meanwood Village Association thanks all the team for their efforts in recording life in Meanwood during that special year.

The Association also wishes to record its thanks to the owners and staff of

FOBI

the shop in the precinct on Green Road, for selling the various books at cost price, as their contribution to the community.

-- -- -- -- -- -- -- -- -- -- -- -- -- -- -- -- -- -- -- --

PAGE INDEX OF PHOTOGRAPHS

"MEANWOOD 2000"

"The village within a city"

In 1999 the committee of the Meanwood Village Association decided to explore the possibilities of a major photographic exercise throughout the Millennium year 2000. This was done by photographing all the buildings in the Parish, and the events, both normal and special, that would be taking place throughout the year.

One of the main "Aims of the Association" as defined in the 1972 constitution is "To record and preserve in all possible ways the history of Meanwood".

A Millennium photographic collection seemed to fit this aim perfectly, so we applied for a National Lottery grant to pay for all the films, processing and printing. We were delighted to receive a cheque for £4,062.00. We also received some grants from Leeds City Council to help to pay for the collecting, copying and archiving of the many photographs.

We decided to call the project **"MEANWOOD 2000"**.

A volunteer team was formed consisting of Paul Bound, Bryn Evans, Brian Glassby, Ian Jackson, John Whalley, Doreen Wood and myself. We divided Meanwood up into 7 areas with each member being responsible for taking photographs of all the buildings in that area.

All the other events etc were allocated to a team member as we went along, and nearly every one was covered by one of us.

With so many photographs coming through it was a major task to collate them all with names, locations and dates. In all we took 127 films of 36 giving a grand total of over 4,500 photographs.

They were all taken on traditional cameras using Kodak 200 Gold print film and were processed by Supasnaps in Headingley.

Two copies of each were printed. One set was mounted on cards for exhibition purposes and the other set lodged with the Leeds City Archive Department at Sheepscar for posterity.

Exhibitions were held in 2001 in the Parochial Hall and in the schoolroom of the Methodist Church and both exhibitions proved very popular.

The first shots were taken just after midnight on January 1st. A few hours later, at the first sunrise of the Millenium, a dash around Meanwood captured it at the Parish Church, King Alfred's Castle and Sugarwell Hill.

Throughout the rest of the year we tried to record something of the many activities taking place at the churches, clubs, schools and other organisations. It was surprising how many things were going on in the area.

As well as organisations we tried to capture the ordinary everyday goings on, and things such as the goods in the shops (with prices).

We also tried to present an honest picture of the area and included rubbish and graffiti, as well as the more glamorous parts.

Time does not stand still of course, and it was surprising how many changes took place during the year. Since 2000 there have been many more and readers will no doubt spot them as they go through the book. For example the The Becketts and the Highbury Works Cricket Club have closed. The original Methodist Church in Church Lane has been converted into modern dwellings, Oddy's Fold on Parkside Road has been refurbished and a new development built alongside it. A large housing development on the old Meanwood Park Hospital site has been completed.

In September 2004 we published Volume 1 of "Meanwood in Pictures" covering the period from 1852 to the 1960s and a year later followed it with Volume 2 taking us from the 1960s to 1999.

Both of these proved extremely popular and copies have been sent all over the world to 'Meanwood exiles'.

In Volumes 1 and 2 the photographs were arranged randomly, but this time, as you will see in the index on page 1, we have placed them into groups.

We have arranged four of the groups into walks, so that if readers wish they can wander around, with book in hand, and see where the photographs were taken, and the changes that have taken place since 2000.

We have included quite a number of dwellings, to show the great variety in the area, ranging from the old stone cottages to the modern styles on the new estates.

It is therefore with great pleasure that we now present Volume 3, containing 330 colour photographs, selected from the Meanwood 2000 project. We hope that readers will add it to their collection of local history to pass on to future generations to enable them to see what life was like in Meanwood in Millennium year.

I wonder what it will be like in the year 3000 ?

Wherever you are in the world I hope you enjoy looking through the pictures as much as we did in taking and presenting them.

Peter Bewell
2007

Note:

We are always pleased to receive photographs, both old and new, to increase our collection. You can either donate them, or lend them to us for copying. Please give dates , names and locations wherever possible. Just contact any of the officers listed on the back page. Thank you.

WALK No. 1

Starting from the Methodist Church at the main crossroads in the centre of Meanwood. (Commonly known as 'the terminus', a name derived from the days when the trams terminated there).

As we leave the Church, heading west down Green Road, we pass the bus shelter, seen here with one of the Black Prince buses.   10th June.

Looking to the left, we see the G.T.Smith superstore which was built on the site of the old Capitol cinema and ballroom (now the Co-op).

The superstore car park, with its variety of cars.

*Inside the store, three happy ladies at the bakery counter. Sue Kingston,
Josi Freer and Elaine Marshall.   19th October.*

Just to the right of the superstore lies the newly opened Veterinary surgery.

6

On the right hand side of the Vets is the Yorkshire Bank, seen here from the outside, the interior and the well used external cash machine. (ATM)

Across the road, on the north side, is the shopping precinct with its wide variety of shops. (Built on the site of the old Bateson's tannery).

Continuing along Green Road, on the right hand side we see Church Avenue climbing up the hill. Built in the 1930s these houses are still as popular as ever. In recent years many of them have added extensions and dormers.

A few yards further along is a seat seen here providing a welcome rest for Doris Wray and Rhoda Child after a shopping expedition.

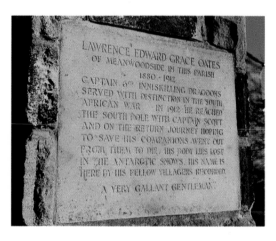

Just behind them on a stone pillar is a memorial tablet commemorating that 'very gallant gentleman', Captain Oates.

Going up towards the church is Memorial Drive. After the First World War this drive was planted on both sides with trees, each of which was in memory of a fallen soldier. In the 1970s the Leeds Federated Housing Association built a number of dwellings on the east side of the drive, some of which are 'sheltered' for elderly residents. Thankfully they managed to retain some of the memorial trees.

Sylvia Philmore and Wendy Pinder out for a stroll. 8th March.

Jenny Creaser, known to many children as 'Aunty Jenny' on her way to visit her mother after a shopping trip. 17th March.

Continuing along Green Road we see the PET SHOP at the bottom corner of Church Lane. In the background is the original Methodist Chapel, occupied by ACORN GLASS (since converted into dwellings).

The next street on the right is Greenwood Mount, with MENZERS newsagent's shop on the bottom corner. (This has also been recently converted into a private house).

The houses in Greenwood Mount showing the popular addition of dormers and P.V.C. windows.

*Going to the top of Greenwood Mount we see a block of flats,
which was originally the Becketts Children's Home.*

*Behind the pillar box the Sunset Road
bungalows rise up the steep hill.*

*Continuing along Green Road we see this
prominent red pillar box on the right.*

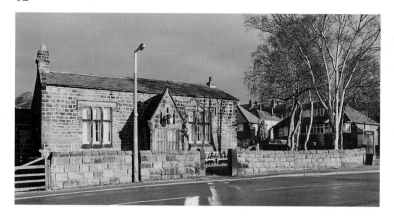

Just beyond Sunset Road stands the Meanwood Institute dating back to the early 19th century. Now a very popular venue for meetings and parties.

Next comes Tannery Square, owned by the Mary Morris Housing Association, which houses overseas married students and their families.

With the advent of mobile phones the public telephone box which stood at the bottom of Sunset Road has since been considered uneconomical and has been removed.   18th October.

Turning into the park a little way further on, we come across Billy the park keeper with his faithful dog. 4th May.

The popular bowling green surrounded by the lovely flower beds tended by Billy.   April.

Further along Green Road stands Meanwood C.of E. Primary School (known to the older generation simply as Green Road School). On the left of the picture is the bottom of the old bell tower, and on the right the old Headmaster's House which now contains the staff room and offices.

On the corner opposite the school stands Ivy Cottage, on this occasion with a group of people from the Headingley Methodist Circuit after a local Treasure Hunt.
25th June.

Down the side of Ivy Cottage runs a ginnel which follows the beck towards Hollin Lane in Headingley.

A little way further on Green Road near the entrance to the car park we come across the Parks Department building and compound (now disused).

Lying in the grass at the far end of the compound is the stone base from a fountain which was originally on Woodhouse Ridge.

Fifty yards or so towards Headingley these old millstones can be seen lying in the beck, a reminder of the area's industrial past.

The tablet on the base of the pillar.

Top: On the far side of the beck stands the memorial pillar to Edwin and Ina Kitson Clark, a very prominent Leeds family and the last private owners of Meanwoodside.

Right: Moving onto the single track road, which winds its way through Meanwood Park, we come across a girl on a pony. 18th April.

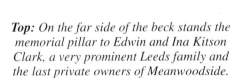

On the left of the road, just before we reach Hustlers Row, we see the beck flowing towards us under a bridge and over a weir. Near the top of the weir some water is diverted into a goit which is a man-made waterway leading to the mills down the valley providing their source of power. The bridge, seen here in the autumn, is on the popular 'Meanwood Valley Trail'.

Left: Hustlers Row is a long line of old cottages formerly occupied by quarrymen and their families. They were quite small, and in some cases owners have converted two of them into one larger dwelling. Seen here are Janet and Paul Matthews with children Nestor and Phoebe at the door of numbers 2 and 3. 18th November.

Below: Continuing along the Meanwood Valley Trail we cross this wooden bridge, seen here with the beck in flood. On the left the ground rises steeply through a wooded area known as The Hollies.   30th October.

Following the footpath we eventually come to the bottom of Dunny Hill. Here we leave the Trail, turn right and start to climb the steep hill. On the left is this large new house and Equestrian Centre.   20th June.

On the right, as we go through the sharp bends, lies Meanwood Grove, another row of old cottages. Seen here is one of the residents Kath Garnett doing her chores.   3rd January.

At the top of the hill, on our right, stands Fairfax, a house with a long and interesting history. It was demolished around 1905 and the stones used to rebuild a new house at right angles to the original. The view here is from the rear of the house.   17th March.

Proceeding along Parkside Road, on the right hand side are the award winning Meanwood Parkside Allotments which are very popular with keen local gardeners. Here is Tony Taylor selling his rhubarb on the Allotments Open Day.   21st May.

On the same day Alan Corners sells some plants to Pauline Tulloch.

Top: *A happy group of allotment holders. Wilf Coy, Geoff Lythe, Alan Lodge, David Catley, Brian Carter, Walter Hartley and Barry Radcliffe.   20th July.*

Left: *Barry Radcliffe at the gate to 'Valhalla'   26th March.*

A little further on is the Meanwood Cricket Club, where cricket has been played for over 100 years. (See Cynthia Ruston's book). May.

FIRE! A scene from the regular bonfire night celebrations at the club.

Team members and supporters outside the pavilion at the special Millennium Day match. Phil Cook, Pete Langley, Mick Dews, Alan Lodge, Colin Murgatroyd, Joan Lodge, Lynn Langley, Walter Burke and Wendy Pinder.

On the left hand side opposite the cricket field are some lovely old cottages, with this one displaying a 1720 datestone over the window.

Spring blossom in front of more old cottages.

A little way further on, just before Oddy's Fold, are these three houses with new porches.

If we walk about 50 yards past the Bay Horse pub a footpath on the left leads us into a new housing estate which has been built on the site of the old Meanwood Park Hospital. Here we can see many of the latest designs of modern houses. The site has been very well landscaped, and there is a footpath all the way round the perimeter of the estate. It is well worth a walk sometime.

Back onto Parkside Road again we see The Bay Horse pub, an old but still very popular drinking and eating place.

Retracing our steps towards the Myrtle pub we can turn left and enter the Holmwood estate. This estate was built in the 1960s on the site of the old Church Farm and a quarry. A wide variety of dwellings of that period can be seen.

Further examples of 1960s housing on the Holmwood estate.

That concludes **WALK No. 1.** *– To get back to the starting point go down through the Holmwoods into Church Lane and at the bottom of the hill is Green Road. Turn left and return to the Methodist Church. Hope you enjoyed this walk.*

MEANWOOD CHILDREN

It's sticky !   A young visitor at the Oddfellows Open Day at the Urban Farm.

Another young lady at the same event. 9th September.

Face painting at the farm.

A cheery looking lad in the shopping precinct.   26th October.

A little angel at the crib service in the Parish Church.   23rd December.

Childhood innocence at the Meanwood C.of E. Primary School B.B.Q.   20th July.

Two happy girls on the Institute wall.   20th April.

Concentration at the Meanwood C.of E. Primary School Summer Fair.   24th June.

Sledging party in Meanwood Park.   28th December.

Skateboarding, a popular pastime with the youngsters.   21st June.

32

Children at Bentley Primary School performing in a Nativity Play.   14th Dec.

Bentley Primary School children in their classroom.   3th June.

Happy diners at Meanwood C.of E. Primary School Parents' Association B.B.Q.   21st. May.

The Mother and Toddler Group who meet in the schoolroom of the Methodist Church on Wednesday afternoons. 8th March.

Children on the edge of the stage during a jumble sale in the Parochial Hall. 21st October.

34

Start of the balloon race at Meanwood C.of E. Primary School. An event which was helping to raise money to fund a new computer suite.   14th April.

WOW! look where mine is going !

A girl and her dog at Meanwood C. of E. Primary School Summer Fair. 24th June.

Children from Meanwood C. of E. Primary School performing a Nativity Play at the Urban Farm. 12th December.

Refreshments time at the Christmas Market in the schoolroom of the Methodist Church. 11th November.

SCHOOLS

Children maypole dancing at the Bentley Primary School Fair.   8th July.

Children in the Bentley Nursery.   13th June.

A lovely little group of children awaiting their turn to perform at the
Bentley School Summer Fair.   8th July.

On the same day some excited children watching the Punch and Judy show.

Important guests at the Bentley Summer Fair. The Lord Mayor of Leeds Councillor Bernard Atha, Harold Best M.P. (an old boy of Bentley Lane School), his wife Glyn and Mrs. Cawsey the headteacher. 8th July.

Staff and pupils of Bentley Primary School at a special service in the Methodist Church. 13th July.

*A group of happy children with their spring flowers at Meanwood
C. of E. Primary School.   24th March.*

More smiles, this time in the classroom.   4th May.

Time for the school dinner.   13th July.

Or, taking the option of your own packed lunch.   13th July.

Jumping for joy!
24th March.

Meanwood C.of E.
Primary School Year 6
children on a
memorable day when
the Rugby League
Challenge Cup was
brought into school by
members of the
victorious Leeds
Rhinos rugby league
team.   3rd March.

Now for something a
little more serious.
Cycling Proficiency
lesson for pupils in the
playground.
22nd June.

42

Children with their Millennium mugs, which were a gift from Leeds City Council.   20th January.

Meanwood C.of E. Primary School. Year 6 and staff having their group photograph taken.   7th June.

Meanwood C.of E. Primary School enjoying the jukebox at the Working Men's Club during a fundraising event. 14th April.

Grandpa and children at the Summer Fair.   24th June.

Reception class children enjoying themselves.   20th September.

The headteacher, Mrs Sanderson and her deputy Mrs. Wedlinscky with some of the children on the May Queen Day. 6th May.

Meanwood C.of E. Primary School jumble sale in the Parochial Hall, organised by the Parent Teacher Association. 21st October.

Centre: *Carr Manor School car boot sale. 14th May.*

Left: *Carr Manor Primary School Summer Fair. 17th June.*

The orchestra practicing at Carr Manor High School. A popular Saturday morning event organised by Leeds City Council under the 'Music for Everyone' scheme.   4th November.

The junior section under the same scheme.

It looks as if a bomb has just dropped ! In fact it is the demolition of the old Cardinal Heenan High School in Tongue Lane.   25th December.

Part of the new Cardinal Heenan High School.   28th December.

The old Schoolmaster's House at Meanwood C.of E. Primary School
which now houses the staff rooms.   4th May.

Carr Manor High School.   9th March.

WALK No. 2

*Starting from the Methodist Church again and proceeding up
Stonegate Road on the left hand side.*

*Carefully crossing the busy road
we commence the walk up the
hill passing this parade of
shops.*

More shops on the parade.

*Next are the Pizza and Tandoori
take-away shops.*

After passing the Working Men's Club we come across houses all the way up the fairly steep hill.

The road then levels out, and we come to the traffic lights at the junction of Parkside Road and Stonegate Road, seen here on a cold winter's day.

Parkland Drive branches off to the left near to this colourful spring blossom.   1st May.

*Go up Parkland Drive a short way and turn to your left into Towers Way to see 'The Towers,' a
fine old building which was converted into flats some years ago.   10th January.*

Continuing up Stonegate Road we see a parade of shops with their distinguishing half-timbered upper storeys.

After leaving the Parklands, the next group of dwellings is the King Alfred's estate.
Seen here is a block of Local Authority flats.

A pair of semi-detached Local Authority houses dating from the nineteen fifties
on the same estate.

Further up Stonegate Road we come to the playing fields on the left. It is well worth the effort of walking across them to the top of the hill from where you can look down upon the new David Lloyd sports complex and the Moortown estate beyond.   24th Nov.

The interior of the sports hall.

We have now reached the top end of the walk. Carefully cross Stonegate Road and start off down the hill. On the left hand side we see a house being extended.

Further down stands Carr Manor, a site with a history dating back several centuries. The present house was constructed in 1881 and has for a number of years been the residence of Judges visiting the City Courts. It is difficult to see the Manor House. This is the stable block.

Top: *As we proceed down the hill towards the traffic lights at the junction with Parkside Road we see, on our left, a large house known as 'Stonegates' which has been converted into flats.*
It is unusual, as the side facing Stonegate Road is plain brickwork, but on the other side, where this photograph was taken, it has a very nice stone façade.

Left: *Beyond the lights is the Alder Hill estate and this eye-catching Lodge with the very prominent chimneys.*

Set back from the main road is another old building, Carr Cottage.

On the left lies an estate of modern private houses, an example of which is seen here in Sycamore Close.

Lower down is the Local Authority/Housing Association estate. These houses are in Stonegate Chase.

We are now back down to
the shopping area. This
archway which stands on
the site of the old Kent
House is at the junction of
Stonegate Road and
Stainbeck Avenue. It is the
pedestrian entrance to the
Northside Shopping Centre,
a complex of large stores
which were built in the
1990s.

Q.L.M. one of the major
stores on the site.

Almost back at the church
we see a variety of premises
from take-aways to these
solicitors' offices.

That concludes **WALK No.2**.
Hope you enjoyed this one
too.

MEANWOOD METHODIST CHURCH

Top: A group of the Brownies.   4th July.

Left: Cathy Barratt the District Commissioner, and leader of the Guides, pictured here with her three daughters.   19th January.

A group of Guides and their leaders.   21st June.

59

*Four smart lads saluting.
8th June.*

*Scouts ready for inspection.
9th June.*

*Leaders of the 8th N.W. Leeds
scouts. Linda Fildes, Duncan
Jeffries, Gillian Marshall, and a
temporary leader from the
University.*

*The congregation at the Harvest Festival Parade Service
in the Methodist Church.   17th September.*

The uniformed groups on the Church steps after the Service.   17th September.

Pauline Daniel and Lily Slade enjoying a joke after the Women's Fellowship meeting. 14th April.

Ron Jeffries hoping to make a sale at the Saturday morning Bric- a- Brac stall.   12th February.

Scouts car washing in the car park for their 'Bob-a-Job' fund raising.   10th June.

Ladies enjoying the Thursday Luncheon Club. 2nd March.

The Vicar, the Revd Richard Wiggen, having refreshments in the schoolroom after the United Good Friday service.   21st April.

The Methodist Minister, the Revd Phil Chilvers, blessing the shoe boxes brought in by the Mother and Toddler Group.
The Shoe Box Appeal is made annually. Gifts are placed in shoeboxes and sent to Eastern Europe for disadvantaged children at Christmas.
22nd November.

Left: Iroko, a Japanese lady living in Leeds for a few years, arranging the flowers in Church. 11ᵗʰ March.

Bottom left: 'Ziggy' the hairdresser, a regular caller after the Thursday Luncheon Club, cutting the hair of Fred Campey in the vestry. 9th March.

Bottom right: George Wiseman, another Thursday regular, departing on his motorised scooter. 2nd March.

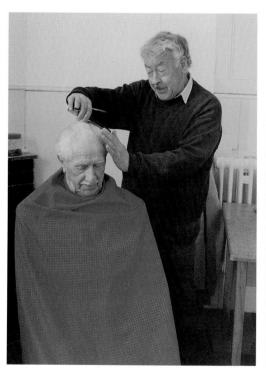

The angels, Margaret Kemp, Marjorie Hopwood and Barbara Turner performing at the Methodist Church Anniversary Concert.   18th March.

The audience seem well pleased !

The first wedding of the Millennium in the Methodist Church.
Lee Christopher Parkinson and Sarah Elizabeth Hamilton.   11th March.

WALK No. 3

Starting again from the Methodist Church, this time going down Monk Bridge Road.

On the right, behind the Cedar Room, we see Arthur Hopwood caring for the environment by binning the rubbish left by others.   29th February.

On the opposite side of the road is this large stone house, viewed from the back.

A little further down the road is the Chinese take-away, in what used to be a fish and chip shop.

Continuing down, we come across a disused shop and these old cottages in Monk Bridge Street.

Turning right along Mill Pond Lane take the unmade footpath to the left and cross this bridge behind the Millside Medical Centre. You come out at the back of the former fellmongers. This was where the wool was taken from animal skins and processed. Commonly known as 'The Tannery'.

The Tannery, including the various workshops and outbuildings, was converted in the late 1990s into quite a large residential area now known as Tannery Park. The development has proved to be a very popular spot with young business people. Here we see a row of cottages on part of the site.

This is a view of the main tannery building from the courtyard. A far cry from the old days when the yard was full of big bales of animal skins. Then, the awful smell from the processing would pervade the whole area.

As part of the development an information centre was created on the site of the old turbine house. Here we see Janice Stone from the developers and Arthur Hopwood the local historian being photographed by a rather uncomfortable pressman.   29th March.

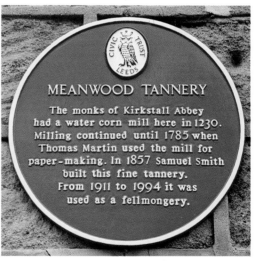

Above: *The Civic Trust plaque which was put in place in 2000.*

Left: *The main archway into the development with the 1857 datestone above and the initials SS which relate to the Samuel Smith named on the plaque.*

Backtrack to Monk Bridge Road. Cross carefully, turn right, and just past the newsagents go down the passageway which eventually comes out into Grove Lane.

You will see on the left this large block of modern flats.

On the right hand side of Grove Lane is The Vale Stables with lots of plants for sale.

Back on the left side again is the Volvo garage.

To the right of the garage is the Vacuum shop at the bottom of Bentley Lane.

Continuing along Grove Lane we pass on the right the car wash and petrol station.
(Now a derelict site).

*Early in the year this building site could be seen at the side of the petrol station.
9th March.*

Later in the year one of the completed houses.   4th Nov.

Retracing our steps, and turning up Bentley Lane, take the first left and you see this cul- de-sac of bungalows in Cross Bentley Lane.

Going up Bentley Lane turn down the first road on the right and just below the school we see this row of houses in Clipstone Avenue.

Just behind Bentley Lane on the left is Bentley Grove.

Continuing up Bentley Lane past this row of terraced houses we reach Meanwood Road. Turn left, and you will soon be back at the Church starting point.

Well done!
*That is **WALK No. 3** completed.*

HOLY TRINITY CHURCH

Millennium awakening for Meanwood !
The bellringers, George Goodchild, William Ogunyinka, Peter Broomfield,
John Whalley, and Kathy Goodchild.   1st January 2000.

A steeplejack climbs the steeple to carry out
repairs. Did you know that there are only 3
clock faces ? Have a look around next
time.   17th September.

The Vicar, the Revd Richard Wiggen lighting
the altar candle on Millennium Day.

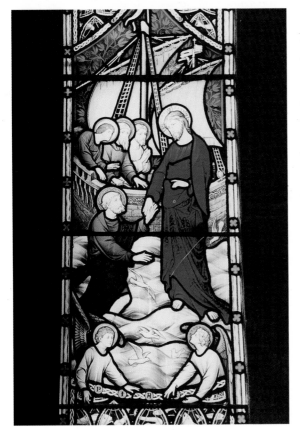

Above: *The congregation after the special Millennium Day service.*

Left: *One of the beautiful stained glass windows.*

76

The retiring Rose Queen, Laura Oxley, reading the lesson.   6th May.

The crowning of the new Rose Queen, Jennifer Brown.

The Rose Queen Jennifer Brown.

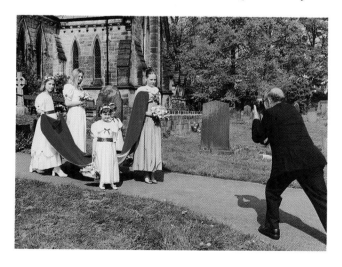

Peter Bewell photographing the Queen and her retinue.

Uniformed leaders. Left to right: Sue Marsden, Susan Houghton, Lynn Cuthbert, Christine Holmes, Mary Harman, Beverley Fox, Lesley Wright and Anne Corners.

The Rainbows' Nativity Play in the Parochial Hall.   6th December.

Raj Kular presenting a cheque to the youth organisations from the estate of the late James Spencer. 1st October.

A group of scouts in the entrance to the Parochial Hall with their Pokeman cards, the latest craze. 12th April.

Children and mums at the Little Mice service. The name is derived from the little mice which can be seen on some of the church oak furniture which was made by the world famous carver and cabinet maker, Thompson of Kilburn.   2nd March.

More of today's Little Mice in the church.   1st October.

The first wedding of the Millennium at Meanwood Parish Church.
Mark Jonathan Horsey to Christina Mary (Tina) Bainbridge.
4th March.

Ladies of the church making a banner in the hall. Lena Sugden, Joan Eales, Sandra Glassby, Rita Jones, Doreen Sykes and Avril Denton.

One of the completed banners hanging in church.

Remembrance Sunday. The wreath bearers, Walter Hall, Mary Dobson and Fred Lockerbie.
12th November.

Elaine Hill, the Meanwood Park Ranger, planting a tree in the churchyard to mark
the new Millennium. (Alas, it didn't survive). 6th May.

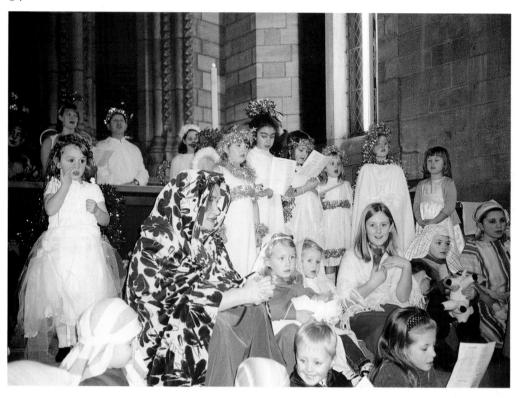

Top: *Children at the altar during the popular Christmas crib service.*
23rd December.

Left: *Aunty Jenny enjoying a cuddle with Santa in the Parochial Hall at the very last session of her playgroup. She had run the group for 27 years.*
19th December.

Facing page: *The Choir in church.*
17th December.

Margaret Fox, Jean Pearson and Marian Reyner enjoying their cream teas in the Hall.
26th August.

A large group of worshippers on Mothering Sunday.   2nd April.

Ladies arranging the flowers for Easter.   22nd April.

*Rosemary Stirk with her daughter Rebecca and granddaughter, on Mothering Sunday.
April 2nd.*

Halloween party in the Parochial Hall. 31st October.

A school jumble sale in the Hall.   4th March.

The ladies exercise class in the Hall.   8th March.

The Vicar enjoying a dance with Vicky Mills at the Rose Queen evening in the Hall.   4th November.

Dancers on the Hall stage the same evening.

The Ogunyinka family performing on African drums in the concert.

SIGNS and NOTICES

The notice board outside the Methodist Church.

Another Methodist notice.

Holy Trinity Church notice board.

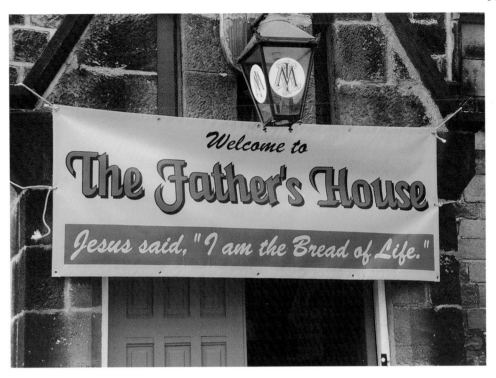

An eye-catching banner outside the Institute where a group of worshippers met regularly.

Church notice at the bottom of Memorial Drive. Regular organ recitals take place in Church during this time.

A grand display of meat in
Ken Stephen's shop in
Meanwood Road. This
butcher's shop closed for
business later in the year
as a result of sustained
competition from the local
supermarkets.
18th October.

'Wineways' shop in
Stainbeck Road.
9th March.

A variety of signs in
Stonegate Road.

Top: *Carwash sign in Grove Lane. 9th March.*

Left: *Petrol prices at the same garage. 9th March.*

Sign for the sale of Fairfax, the old house in Parkside Road.   26th December.

The refreshments van for the workers on the new school in Tongue Lane. On the right is the sign for the sale of land on the old Meanwood Park Hospital site.   12th January.

The two taverns on Parkside Road. The Bay Horse and The Myrtle.

Art or Graffiti? I will let the reader decide. Garage wall décor behind Grove Lane.

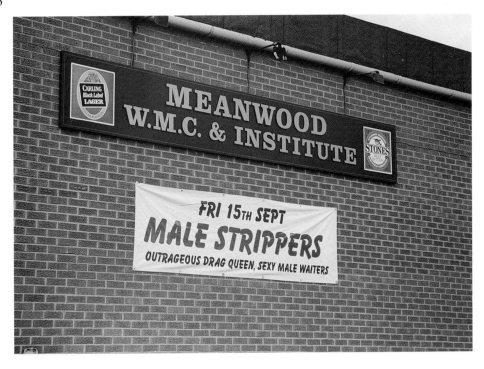

The saucy section. (The Working Men's Club and the bus shelter). No further comments!

97

*Children carrying banners
in Church on Womens'
World Day of Prayer.
March 3rd.*

Inside the Burger King.

Signs in Stonegate Road.

THE MEANWOOD VILLAGE ASSOCIATION

Quiz Night at the Parochial Hall.
Doreen Wood, Janet Pouncey, Betty Shoesmith, Frank Dunderdale, Pat Auton and
Mavis Prentice.   12th February.

More contenders. Bryn and Sylvia Evans, Diana and Tony Hutton, and Anne and Iain Burgess.

Members of the Association outside the Meanwood Institute just prior to setting off on the traditional Easter Tuesday walk.   25th April.

Members of the Committee outside the Institute.
Front row: *Cathy Stevens, Peggy Palmer, Jill Laurillard, Doreen Wood, Jackie Brewer, Val Milner, and Anne Burgess.*
Back row: *Peter Bewell, Ken Palmer, Roy Hall, Chris Needham, Peter Chamley, Harrison Mattinson, Arthur Hopwood and Bryn Evans.   April.*

THE MEANWOOD INSTITUTE

Top: Ladies of the Women's Institute.   20th May.

Left: Women's Institute coffee morning.   20th May.

Janet Pouncey planting the Millennium Wisteria on the same day. (It has since flourished).

Top: Mrs Robinson at her 90th birthday celebrations chatting to her sister, Mabel Perfect. 18th November.

Left: Constance Pape, Christine Bulmer and Rita Durrant busy at the needlework class which meets weekly in the Meanwood Institute. 22nd June.

A display of their work at a fund raising morning. 28th October.

The committee of the Meanwood Institute invite some of the older residents in Meanwood to what has been named as a 'Tea and Chat' on a Sunday afternoon, several times a year. As well as refreshments, some form of entertainment is arranged. Transport is provided for those who need it.
In this photograph the choir from Meanwood C. of E. Primary School are entertaining at Christmas.

There is usually a free raffle. Seen here is the Chairman of the Institute Committee Peter Smithson drawing the lucky ticket and Jackie Brewer ready with the prizes.   14th May.

Enjoying the refreshments are Mrs Mitton, Mrs Thomas, Freda Wilks, Annie Hinchcliffe and Mr Taylor.   14th May.

A grand display of vegetables and flowers at the Meanwood Parkside Allotments Association Annual Show.
2nd September.

Trevor Gadsby receiving his award.

Happy visitors to the show, Christine Bewell and her mother Bessie.

*The Institute committee.
Front; Cathy Stevens, Peter
Smithson (chairman) and
Jackie Brewer. Middle; Roy
Tulloch, George
Cockrill,Teresa Metcalfe, Tony
Taylor. Back; Harold
Bradbury, Peter Bewell, Jim
Durrant, and Pete Spedding.
4th May.*

*One of the popular 'Pate &
Plonk' Sunday lunches.
Alan Taylor, Marjorie Taylor,
Arthur Barber, Shirley Barber,
Dorothy Walsh, Pauline
Tulloch and Kay Smithson.
18th June.*

*Frank Dunderdale, giving a talk about his collection of
teaspoons.   11th September.*

Millennium party for members of the committee and their partners.

Anne Burgess, Iain Burgess, Christine Bewell, Rita Durrant, Peter Bewell, Jim Durrant, Sylvia Evans and Bryn Evans. 21st January.

Cheers ! Same party, Peter Smithson, Roy Tulloch, Pete Spedding, Pat Spedding, Kay Smithson and Pauline Tulloch.

Mike Osbourne giving some snooker tuition to Kirsty Fildes. 26th April.

WALK NO. 4 DOWN MEANWOOD ROAD

The first building on this walk is the The Becketts public house on the corner on the right.
(Demolished in 2007).

On the opposite side of the road is this row of shops which have changed hands several times
over the years.

Staying on the right hand side, the Post Office stands in the centre of the row of shops. The interior is shown here.

A little further on is a pair of what used to be large houses. The right hand one was for many years the Yorkshire Penny Bank and then a doctor's surgery.

This more modern building, now the Lloyds Pharmacy, was a Supermarket in 2000.

Opposite the supermarket is the Meanwood Health Centre, and here is Dr Andrew Newbound, the senior partner of the practice.   12th May.

Not usually as quiet as this! The waiting room.   12th May.

Take a diversion now up Bentley Lane, and on the left hand side is this three storey block of flats.

On the other side is Bentley Court, a sheltered housing scheme operated by the Anchor Housing Association.

A bit off route, but at the back of Bentley Court lies the Community Centre. One of the various activities centred here is the gardening club. Shown here is the leader of the club planting a Millennium Tree.

Back now into Meanwood Road. This stone house called 'The Poplars' has since been demolished. A complex of modern flats now stands on the site.

Some of the three rows of terrace houses, many of which are occupied by students and have had dormers added.

Just behind the terrace houses on the right is Bentley Primary School, which used to house the library. Here is Christine Bewell having a laugh with Helen the librarian. Both the school and library have since been closed.
12th February.

*Carry on down to the traffic lights and turn left up Stainbeck Road
where you will see on the right Kingdom Hall.*

A little further on, just past the crossroads, is this dental practice and a row of shops.

Retracing our steps to the traffic lights we rejoin Meanwood Road and head towards town. On the right is this litter strewn track which leads to the Bus Vale rugby ground.

Just past this there is the modern estate named the Boothroyds which was built on the site of Yorkshire Switchgear, a major local employer in days past.

Another show house on the site.

Crossing over to the left, we see this sign for the farm.

Go up Farm Hill, take the first turning on the right Sugarwell Road,
and see these Local Authority bungalows and houses.

Further along was this display of flowers outside a house
where there had been a murder.   19th April.

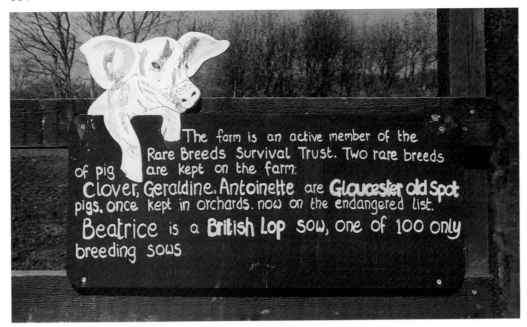

The farm is an active member of the Rare Breeds Survival Trust. Two rare breeds of pig are kept on the farm: Clover, Geraldine, Antoinette are Gloucester Old Spot pigs, once kept in orchards, now on the endangered list. Beatrice is a British Lop sow, one of 100 only breeding sows

At the end of this road lies the Urban Farm. This is a very popular venue for families, as they can see all kinds of farm animals. Visitors can also wander around areas used for growing a variety of crops, flowers and other plants.

One of the farm helpers and Caroline Bewell feeding the ducks.   19th April.

*The Epicentre, which opened in 1999. A high-tech structure with an
environmentally friendly turf roof, and many other interesting features.*

*The Kirkstall Valley Rangers demonstrating the art of besom making on an Open Day
(An old method of making sweeping brushes from twigs).   21st May.*

*Back to Farm Hill South. A little way further up on the right was the Model Farm Riding Centre.
It did sterling work for young people, including the disabled, but sadly has had to close
following the death of Joyce Gosson who ran the project. Seen in this picture is a group setting
off on a pony trek.   30th April.*

A happy group at the stables.   19th April.

This shot taken from Farm Hill Rise shows in the background Woodhouse Ridge, which has changed considerably over the last 50 or 60 years, from an open landscape of pleasant paths, shelters and a bandstand to a densely wooded hillside.   30th May.

Back on the Urban Farm is Margaret Lickess of the Oddfellows and Bernard Atha the Lord Mayor, on the Farm 'Fun Day'.   9th September.

THE MEANWOOD MEN'S SOCIETY

At the annual snooker tournament in the Institute. Jack Mathers, Bryn Evans, Eric Endersby, Keith Denney, Roy Tulloch, Tony Taylor and Jim Durrant.   14th February.

One of the regular Monday evening meetings of the society held in the cricket pavilion at Highbury Works. (Since closed).   17th April.

The Spedding family enjoying some lunch on the Family Christmas Walk.   27th December.

The full party on the walk, which went into the Wharfe valley from Bramhope.   27th December.

The Annual Dinner at the Mansion in Roundhay Park. Roy and Pauline Tulloch,
Peter and Kay Smithson, Alan and Marjorie Taylor, Tony and
Margaret Taylor, Alan and Carol Smith.   16th June.

THE HELPERS   (Where would we be without them?)

Audrey Taylor, Cathy Holding, Anne Fairy and Sylvia Philmore serving at the Institute at the 'Tea and Chat' afternoon.   14th May.

Sheila Stephenson and Barbara Blakeney serving the wine at the Church Wine Walk. This popular summer's evening event started in the early nineties as a fundraising effort for M.S.B.A. (The Meanwood School Building Appeal). These walks have been held regularly ever since, as a very sociable way of raising funds.   24th June.

Jean Cooper, Iroko, Jan Chilvers, and Alice Lowry in the kitchen at the Methodist schoolroom on the regular Saturday Coffee Morning.   12th February.

Alison Wilson and Pat Spedding enjoying their work in the Parochial Hall kitchen at the Guides Concert Evening.   14th July.

Jean Carter and Jean Shillito in the Institute kitchen during the Flower and Vegetable Show.   2nd September.

Shirley Hoyland, with Brian and Sandra Glassby preparing a Parish Breakfast.   8th October.

*Doris Spence, Dorothy Carroll, Lily Slade and Brenda Binge working in the Methodist Church Kitchen for the Thursday Luncheon Club.
2nd March.*

*Lesley Wright and Beverley Fox getting the tea ready at the Parents' and Governors' meeting in Meanwood C.of E. Primary School.
14th April.*

Jim Durrant busy redecorating the Institute front doors. 15th June.

MISCELLANEOUS

Sue Gallie, the manager of MENA (Meanwood Elderly Neighbourhood Action)
in her office at the Community Centre on Stainbeck Avenue.
They do excellent work for the older residents of Meanwood.

A Saturday morning in Meanwoodside. A team of volunteer workers from the Meanwood Village
Association clearing the old pond. Jackie Brewer, Anne Burgess and Roy Hall.

*Interesting patterns in the early morning sunshine. The snowy playground
in Meanwoodside before the children arrive!   29th February.*

*A fascinating display of architectural features on
Meanwood Towers off Stonegate Road.*

The latest in youths' footwear. Carr Manor Primary School Summer Fair.   17th June.

Sale time in the shoe shop.   18th October.

*The latest road
sweeper in
Green Road.*

*A bigger
version in
Church
Avenue.*

*Refuse collection
vehicle in
Towers Way.*

The modern version of the 'Rag & Bone Man' in Parkland Drive.   9th May.

Jackie Brewer, Susan Atkinson and Sheila Stephenson enjoying their ice cream on a
church outing.   15th June.

A fast disappearing sight. The home delivery milkman.   19th October.

Fish delivery man in Church Avenue.   12th June.

Volunteer litter pickers on Parkside Road, organised by Councillor Brenda Lancaster who is standing on the right. 11th March.

It is not the genuine article! It was a temporary gravestone erected in the churchyard for the Yorkshire Television series of 'A TOUCH OF FROST'.

Malinee Brown who organised a party at her house in Holmwood Avenue to raise funds for a school in her home village in Thailand.   27th August.

Voting day. Annie Hinchcliffe giving Christine Bewell her voting slip in the Parochial Hall Polling Station, with Barbara Blakeney looking on.   4th May.

Videos for sale in the 'Star Video' shop.

Arthur Hopwood giving a talk about Meanwood at the Bentley Library.   12th January.

Utter concentration from the ladies in the computer class at the Community Centre. 13th June.

Rest time at the Tea Dance in the Community Centre. 13th September.

Also in the Community Centre, the Ladies keep fit class. 14th June.

Bywater Farm cottages, which are on the far side of the RingRoad.   20th June.

Runners in the Leeds Half Marathon passing the terminus.   14th April.

A reminder of the area's history in quarrying. Stones seen in the old quarry near the Myrtle Tavern.

Pete Spedding making a purchase from Jackie Brewer at the
Meanwood C.of E. Primary School Summer Fair.   24th June.

A group of young people in the Meanwood C.C. pavilion .   5th November.

137

Staff at the bar in the Myrtle Tavern.   20th November.

Alan Smith, Pete Smithson and Tony Taylor at a Myrtle Quiz Night.   20th November.

Furniture for sale outside a shop in Stainbeck Road.   18th March.

Discarded goods at the Meanwood Road reclamation centre. (Known in the past as 'The Destructor' with its massive chimney, where most of the area's rubbish was burnt).

Sarah Challenor with her girls at the Methodist Church Pancake Lunch.   7th March.

Fiona and Caroline Bewell at the Urban Farm chicken house.   19th April.

Michelle Sutcliffe, the Ladies World Flyweight Boxing Champion proudly displaying her belt. 2nd March.

Evelyn Danby, a lady who lived in three centuries ! She was born on 4th September 1897 in the Highburys and attended Green Road school from the age of 3. At 103 thought to be the oldest Meanwood lady living in 2000. 18th September.

Two delightful little attendants at the Rose Queen Day at the Church.   4th April.

Carr Manor School music class.   4th November.

Meanwood C.of E. Primary School Summer Fair.   24th June.

All the latest Pokemon games in the Burger King.   April.

Arthur Barber welcoming visitors to the open day at the Urban Farm on the Oddfellows Fun Day.   9th September.

Thankfully no customers for these happy St. John's Ambulance first aiders at the same event.

Frank Dunderdale enjoying a joke with the Rose Queen and her retinue in the church grounds. 4th April.